Presented by

London's
Publishing Company

BRIAN E. CLARK

This book is dedicated to my daughter
London M. Clark

Being good at sports is COOL, but being good at other things is also cool.

Think about it. And list everything that you are good at or things that you would like to be good at. For example, you may be good at drawing, ice skating or cooking.

_____

_____

_____

It's COOL to brush your teeth and floss, because Nobody likes cavities and bad breath.

Think about it. How often do you brush and floss your teeth? Do you think that's enough?

_____

_____

_____

It's COOL to listen to your parents, because they love you.

Think about it. Do you ALWAYS listen to what your parents tell you?

_____

_____

_____

3

It's COOL to be called a nerd, because nerds grow up to be COOL, RICH and SUCCESSFUL.

Think about it. Have you ever been called a Nerd? How did it make you feel? Have you ever called another kid a nerd? What were you really trying to say?

_____

_____

_____

It's COOL to be a leader, and it is NOT COOL to be a follower.

Think about it. Are you a leader or a follower? If you are a follower, how can you improve and become a leader?

_____

_____

_____

5

It's COOL to be different from other kids.

Think about it. Are you JUST like everyone else, or are you your own person?

_____

_____

_____

It's COOL to tell your family and friends that you love them.

Think about it. Do you love your family and friends? Do you tell them you love them?

_____

_____

_____

It's COOL to listen to the music you like.

Think about it. Do you listen to the music you like to hear, or do you listen to music that other people like to hear because you want to fit in?

_____

_____

_____

No matter what shoes or clothes you have on, you are still cool.

Think about it. Do you have to wear the same clothes and shoes as other kids? Or are you still COOL with the things you wear?

_____
_____
_____

It's COOL to read books, because reading teaches you things that make you even COOLER.

Think about it. Do you like to read books? Why or why not?

_____
_____
_____

It's COOL to be nice to your sisters and brothers.

Think about it. Are you nice to your brothers and sisters or could you be nicer?

_____
_____
_____

It's COOL to have manners and say "Please" and "Thank you".

Think about it. Do you have good manners?

It's COOL to have friends of all colors, shapes, and sizes because we are all COOL.

Think about it. Do you have friends who look different from you? If not, make a new and different friend. How do you plan to do that?

_____
_____
_____

It's COOL to wear glasses, because they are a part of you.

Think about it. Do other kids tease you for wearing glasses? If so, how does it make you feel? How do you feel about kids that wear glasses?

_____

_____

_____

It's COOL to stick up for someone else who is being picked on, because bullying is NOT COOL.

Think about it. Are you a bully? Are you being bullied? Do you know anyone who is being bullied? If so, what will you do about it? Will you tell an adult?

_____

_____

It's COOL to make good grades, because your teachers and parents will be soooo proud of you.

Think about it. Are your grades as high as you want them to be? If not, why? What can you do to raise your grades higher?

_____

_____

_____

It's cool to wear your hair differently from other kids.

Think about it. Do you wear your hair like others?

_____
_____
_____

It's COOL to have big dreams and goals in life.

Think about it. What are your biggest dreams in life? What do you want to be when you grow up?

_____

_____

_____

It's COOL to be you, because you are COOL.

Think about it. Do you believe that you are a COOL kid?

_____

_____

_____

19

Now Scream (Unless you are in a library)

I pledge,

To always be myself, because I am cool. I define what is cool. I will always remember that being smart is cool. And I am a smart and great kid. It's cool to do my best in everything that I do, and I will always do so. I am confident that I am cool. And I will always do what's cool for me, no matter what other kids think.

(Your name)_____

This book is a 1st edition book written by myself, Brian E. Clark and my goal in life is to make this world a better place.

Made in United States
Orlando, FL
02 December 2021